THE BIBLE
SIMPLIFIED

BY JOHN H. MILLER

ISBN: 979-8-9924813-0-3 (Paperback)
          979-8-9924813-1-0 (E-book)

Library of Congress Control Number: 2025902201

Published By:

Texarkana, TX
www.churchontherock.org

Publisher Provider:

CONTENTS

"It is impossible to rightly govern the world without the Bible."

—George Washington

"The Bible is the best book in the world. It contains more …than all the libraries I have seen."

—John Adams

"The Bible makes the best people in the world."

—Thomas Jefferson

"So great is my veneration for the Bible, that the earlier my children begin to read it the more confident will be my hopes that they will prove useful citizens to their country and respectable members of society."

—John Quincy Adams

"I believe the Bible is the best gift God has ever given to man. All the good from The Savior of the world is communicated to us through this Book."

—Abraham Lincoln

"The Bible is the Anchor of our liberties."

—Ulysses S. Grant

"No educated man can afford to be ignorant of the Bible."

—Theodore Roosevelt

"A thorough knowledge of the Bible is worth more than a college education."

—Theodore Roosevelt

"The Bible is the one supreme source of revelation of the meaning of life."

—Woodrow Wilson

"The whole of the inspirations of our civilization springs from the teachings of Christ... to read the Bible... is a necessity of American life."

—Herbert Hoover

"We rest with assurance upon the impregnable rock of Holy Scripture."

—Winston Churchill

"Fellow prisoners held the Bible and turned the pages for me because my fingers were so crushed that I could not use them. I read the Bible, and I have read it the rest of my life."

—Syngman Rhee

"Believe me, sir, never a night goes by, be I ever so tired, but I read the Word of God before I go to bed."

—Douglas MacArthur

"The Bible is a book in comparison with which all others in my eyes are of minor importance, and in which in all my perplexities and distresses has never failed to give me light and strength."

—Robert E. Lee

"If you are ignorant of God's Word, you will always be ignorant of God's will."

—Billy Graham

"Inside every one of us we have something tugging at us, telling us to believe in something…(the Bible) is the answer to that."

—Denzel Washington

"The volume of Scriptures… reveal the will of God."

—Sir Francis Bacon

"We account the Scriptures of God to be the most sublime philosophy. I find more sure marks of authenticity in the Bible than in any profane history whatsoever."

—Sir Isaac Newton

"In sickness or in health, one can find comfort and constructive advice in the Bible."

—Charles W. Mayo

"I believe the Scriptures of the Old and New Testament to be the will and the Word of God."

—Daniel Webster

"Young men, my advice to you is that you cultivate an acquaintance with, and a firm belief in, the Holy Scriptures."

—Benjamin Franklin

"This is a Book worth more than all the others that were ever printed."

—Patrick Henry

"It is impossible to mentally or socially enslave a Bible-reading people."

—Horace Greeley

"The existence of the Bible as a book for the people is the greatest benefit which the human race has ever experienced."

—Immanuel Kant

"It has God for its Author, salvation for its end, and truth, without any mixture of error, for its matter: it is all pure, sincere, nothing too much, nothing wanting."

—John Locke

"Without the Bible the education of a child in the present state of society is impossible."

—Count Leo Tolstoy

"It is the best Book that ever was or ever will be in the world."

—Charles Dickens

"The Bible is the unfailing guide which points the way for men to the perfect life."

—J. Edgar Hoover

"In the Bible I find a confidence mightier than the utmost evil."

—Helen Keller

"When you align yourself with God's purpose as described in the Scriptures, something special happens to your life."

—Bono

"Put your nose into the Bible everyday. It is your spiritual food and then share it. Make a vow not to be a lukewarm Christian."

—Kirk Cameron

"You've got to work the Word for the Word to work."

—Sadie Robertson

"I'm in my bible every day, like that's absolutely been getting me through everything… That's really where the source of truth is for me."

—Candace Cameron Bure

Many of the quotes above were found in the article: Willmington, Harold, "Statements from Famous Personalities Concerning the Bible" (2018). The Owner's Manual File. 72.
https://digitalcommons.liberty.edu/owners_manual/72

PREFACE

I grew up in church and my mother gave me a copy of the Bible, but I never read it. It sat on a bookshelf in my bedroom for years. When I was 19 years old, I was searching for God and didn't realize it. Unbeknownst to me, God was watching over my life and sent a Gideon to give me a copy of a Bible. I made it a goal while I was in the Navy that I would read through the whole Bible. One night, sitting on my bunk in boot camp, I found a plan of salvation in the back of a Gideons Bible. I remember it as if it was yesterday. As I read the Bible, I realized how much God loves me and had a plan for my life. I received Jesus Christ as my Lord and Savior, and made it my life-long ambition to read and study His Word.

The Bible has been the most influential book in my life. It has shaped my values and priorities. It has changed the way I act and think and it's eternal truths can change you as well. I try to read the Bible every day and ask God to show me how the Bible applies to my everyday life. I ask Him to show areas that I need to grow in, attitudes that I need to change, actions that I need to take. The Word of

God is relevant today. No matter how many times I may read the Bible, God seems to speak to me every time. I believe He will do the same for you.

The purpose of this booklet is to explain to you how the 66 individual books of the Bible form a cohesive whole and convey a central message about the person of Jesus Christ.

I pray that as you read through this booklet, you will embrace a fresh understanding and appreciation of the most important book ever written. I also pray that you will open your heart just like I did as a 19 year old teenager to the teachings of Scripture and that you will allow God to give you a better life now that will last for all eternity.

1

What's So Amazing about the Bible?

Washington, D.C. is a city filled with iconic buildings. Dotting the landscape of America's capital are structures made of brick and marble that testify to the historic nature of this world-renown city, and to the country she represents.

However, nestled among the thousands of government buildings and edifices is a very unique building. It's called "The Museum of the Bible." Built at a cost of approximately half a billion dollars, this museum stands eight stories tall, occupies some 430,000 square feet of space, and is filled with valuable artifacts and treasures. Although elaborate, the reason for this museum is simple: to tell the world about a book called "The Bible." But why would so much money be spent on such a museum? Why would an entire museum be dedicated to one book? Part of the answer is found in the fact that the Bible is the most important book in all of human history. The Bible is the most copied, printed, distributed, quoted, referenced, and most digitized book since the invention of the printing press, and even before. It still holds the top spot in publishing as the #1 Bestselling Book of All Time. And even today, it continues to outsell every other book, with over 100 million copies sold *every year*.[1]

And the Christian group, The Gideons, give away, on average, two Bibles every second of every day across the world.

While these stats might help explain the popularity of this book, there is another reason for the Bible's unparalleled worldwide success and reach. Simply put, it is the very Word of God Himself. A written revelation from the Creator to His creation. And that includes *you*.

Second Timothy provides a framework for viewing the Bible:

> You have been taught the holy Scriptures from childhood, and they have given you the wisdom to receive the salvation that comes by trusting in Christ Jesus. All Scripture is inspired by God and is useful to teach us what is true and to make us realize what is wrong in our lives. It corrects us when we are wrong and teaches us to do what is right. (2 Timothy 3:15–16 NLT)

This, then, is **the ultimate purpose of the Bible—to show you and I how we can be delivered from the power of sin and eternal judgment, and experience salvation by trusting in Christ alone.**

---

[1] https://www.economist.com/christmas-specials/2007/12/19/the-battle-of-the-books

That same passage tells us that "all Scripture" is inspired by God. The word "inspired" literally means "God-breathed," and signifies that the Holy Spirit internally moved men, causing them to write the Bible in their particular historical, cultural, and geographical context, as well as in their own language of the day. And yet, despite being written so long ago, the Bible continues to profoundly speak to us in our day. It teaches us what is true in an age when truth is considered to be fluid and changing. It helps us realize what is wrong in our lives and our hearts, and how to make them whole again. The Bible contains God's perspective on what is right and wrong. According to Scripture, right and wrong are not determined by individual preference, personal philosophy, majority vote, the voice of politicians or the opinion of an expert, but rather by God's Word alone.

> Like a recurring theme or a musical refrain, there is a repeating Thread of Redemption running throughout the 66 books of the Bible.

This logically makes sense if the Bible really is the Creator's revelation to mankind. And that's what it claims to be ... the literal *word* of God.

You can look at the Bible as a single story that begins in Genesis and continues through Revelation. Throughout this little book, you will discover the central message of Scripture. Like a recurring theme or a musical refrain, there is a repeating Thread of Redemption running throughout the 66 books of the Bible. It tells us how God, through Jesus Christ, has restored the separation between Himself and humanity. Far more than merely an ancient document, God's word speaks to modern society and culture today just like it did to those to whom it was originally written. It can do this because its truths are timeless and "alive" (Hebrews 4:12). And because it's from God, it's also authoritative and binding upon mankind.

It reminds me of the old children's song, "The B.I.B.L.E." which goes:

> The B.I.B.L.E.
> Yes, that's the book for me
> I stand alone on the word of God
> The B.I.B.L.E.

As you read, I hope you gain a new *perspective* and appreciation of the Bible. That Book in your hand is about 1,800 pages, all told. That's a lot of book! It's a story covering some 4,000 years of history, even extending into eternity. But don't feel overwhelmed. My goal is to help you understand how it all fits together. I want to help you understand how the pieces of the puzzle come together to form a beautiful portrait of love and hope from God to you.

2

The Old Testament - Someone is Coming

Let's begin with some overall Bible facts. The Bible is like a library made up of 66 books which were written by about 44 authors over a period of 1500 to 2000 years. It tells the story of God and His relationship with humankind. There are two major divisions, or sections, in the Bible: the Old Testament (before Christ came) and the New Testament (after Christ came). The word "testament" actually means *covenant*. So, the Bible reveals God's covenant between Himself and humanity.

The way we understand (and interpret) the Old Testament is through the New Testament. For example, if you just randomly opened your Bible and read in Leviticus that someone is making an animal sacrifice for their sin, you might think, "Well, it's in the Bible, so maybe I should also do that so God will forgive my sin too." However, the New Testament tells us that Jesus Christ died in order to permanently remove the penalty of your sin (Romans 6:23; Hebrews 7:24–25; 10:1–4, 10–14). We also learn from the New Testament that those Old Testament animals were sacrificed to temporarily cover sin until the ultimate and final sacrifice could be made. By themselves, those sacrifices could never take away the stain and guilt of our sin (1 Peter 1:18–19; Hebrews 10:4). So, we read the Old through the lens of the New.

The biblical story takes place primarily in the Middle East, particularly in the nation of Israel, though it also spills over into Egypt and Africa. It makes its way into Asia Minor too, traveling westward toward Italy and Spain. The Bible literally covers the whole Mediterranean world.

In the Old Testament, God's people are called the Jews. In the New Testament, God's chosen people are called Christians, or collectively referred to as the "Church," meaning the "called out ones." The most important character in the Bible, however, is obviously God Himself.

God desires a relationship with the people He created. Put more specifically and personally, God wants a relationship with *you*.

But what is the overall message of this great Book? This single book has captured the attention of humanity since it was completed, and has shaped the foundation and development of civilization. Its central, unifying theme is this:

God desires a relationship with the people He created. Put more specifically and personally, God wants a relationship with *you*.

Sometimes we view the Bible as being this untouchable, holy book, surrounded with hush and awe. We can almost become a bit superstitious about it, or think it should only be used in religious liturgy and church services. But the Bible is more than just a religious Book. It actually opens the door for a real and dynamic relationship with the God Who made us.

Not long ago, my wife and I celebrated the birth of our first grandchild. And from the moment he arrived at our house, there was a tug of war between us to see who would get to hold this little baby. "I'm holding him now … No, *I'm* holding him … It's my turn!" And as soon as he left to go visit his other set of grandparents, I began texting my daughter-in-law, Brittany:

Me: does he miss me?
Brittany: yes.
Me: does he miss me the most?
Brittany: of course.

I couldn't get enough of that little guy. I wanted one more picture: another chance to be with him, to see a video of him. I wanted to be with him. I wanted a *relationship* with him.

I believe God wants that kind of relationship with you. And that's why He is pursuing you. You see, the Bible is not just a list of commandments from an angry God who can't wait to punish you when you mess up. It's a Book about a God who wants a loving relationship with you.

Because He loves you.

However, as we look at this entire biblical story, we encounter a problem. A big one. Scripture tells us that sin entered into the human race through Adam and Eve, separating us from God. All the evil that we know in the world today, along with all its heartache, came because of sin. The rest of the Bible is the story of God repairing, redeeming, and restoring that broken relationship between Himself and us. While we were separated from Him, God built a bridge over that sin chasm through Jesus Christ so that we could know Him, enjoy Him, and spend an eternity with Him in a very real place called Heaven.

That is the story of the Bible.

But stepping back a bit, let's get a further "Drone's Eye View" of the Bible. There are 39 books in the Old Testament. And within those, there are four major divisions:

The Pentateuch, (or the Law of Moses) which contains the first five books of the Bible (*Penta* = five, and *teuch*= law). The Pentateuch includes Genesis, which recounts creation and the early history of the Jews. Actually, if you wanted to simplify the entire Old Testament (which is about two-thirds of the Bible), you could view Genesis as the book of beginnings as well as the history of the Jewish people. Through the Jewish people, we were given the law of Moses, and that's where we find the Ten Commandments. Through the history of the Jewish people we also see the ancestry of Christ. The first pages of Matthew's and Luke's Gospels help us trace the lineage of Jesus all the way back to Adam. So, that's the Pentateuch. The first five books.

The Old Testament continues with the history of Israel, made up of 12 books (Joshua, Judges, Ruth, First and Second Samuel, First and Second Kings, First and Second Chronicles, Ezra, Nehemiah, and Esther). These books describe how obedience or disobedience to the Covenant, the Law of Moses, brought either blessing or judgment on the nation of Israel.

Following this, there are the "writing books," or books of poetry. There are five of these. Most people are somewhat familiar with Psalms and Proverbs. Both books are rooted in the concept that the fear of the Lord is the beginning of wisdom. But this category also includes Job, Ecclesiastes, and Song of Solomon.

The Bible has never been more accessible than it is today.

The Bible has never been more accessible than it is today. There are numerous Bible apps to help you engage the Scriptures digitally, providing daily reading suggestions and even study guides. For example, let's say you wanted to read the Bible every day for a month. Where would you begin? I would suggest a good place to start would be in the book of Proverbs. This book has 31 chapters, one for each day of the month. Another source of wisdom is Ecclesiastes, written by Solomon, the wisest man who ever lived. After trying everything in life to be happy—education, experiences, achievements, pleasure, architecture, knowledge—he said this:

> Now all has been heard;
> here is the conclusion of the matter:
> Fear God and keep his commandments,
> for this is the duty of all mankind.
> For God will bring every deed into judgment,
> including every hidden thing,
> whether it is good or evil.
> (Ecclesiastes 12:13–14 niv)

This is the kind of wisdom worth passing on to your kids, grandkids, other relatives, and friends. If you are lying on your deathbed, and your family is gathered around you, don't you think God's wisdom is a better legacy to leave rather than human understanding? There are many things that are important in this life, but there are none greater than the ultimate priorities found in God and His wisdom. And the Bible's books of poetry contain those priorities.

Next we encounter what are known as the Prophetic books. These include five major prophets and 12 minor prophets. The main difference between the major and the minor prophets is their length. For example, Isaiah is much longer than Naham or Habakkuk. Within these books we discover the message of God's prophets. The timeline of the prophets covers the 700 years from when Moses gave the law up until the time of God's people's return from exile. These prophets called the Jewish people back to God after they had strayed. If they were in trouble, found themselves in a mess, or were sinning, the prophets would urge them to repent and to get back on track so that God's blessings would follow. But the most important thing that the prophets did was to predict the future, specifically about the coming Messiah, Jesus Christ.

It has been suggested that there are some 300 prophecies, or predictions, in the Old Testament. These were made hundreds of years before Jesus Christ was born, and they foretell Christ's birth, life, death, and resurrection. One prophecy in particular, Micah 5:2, even prophesies the exact location of His birth. From this small Judean village, Bethlehem, the Messiah and Deliverer of Israel would come. And when you read Matthew's Gospel account, some 800 years later, guess where Jesus was born?

In Bethlehem, of course (see Matthew 2:2).

I realize that some readers may not identify as Christian. In fact, you may even be quite skeptical about the claims of the Bible. If so, I would ask you to consider doing an in-depth study of the writings of the prophets concerning the coming Messiah, prophecies made hundreds of years before the birth of Christ. The mathematical odds of these prophecies being fulfilled are astronomical. The chance of just eight of these prophecies being fulfilled by one man are mind-blowing. Consider this: Cover the whole state of Texas one foot deep in silver dollars. Then mark one of those silver dollars and mix it up among the rest. Then blindfold a person and let them pick one silver dollar from across the entire state of Texas. The chances that they would pick the marked silver dollar on the first try are the same odds as one person fulfilling just eight of those Old Testament prophecies. Jesus fulfilled them all. That by itself is convincing proof of the deity of Jesus Christ. It also is further evidence of how amazing the Bible is.

3

In the Beginning...

Now, let's rewind for a minute to the book of Genesis. Genesis is called the "book of beginnings." The very first verse in Genesis chapter 1 makes a bold claim:

"In the beginning, God created the heavens and the earth" (Genesis 1:1 ESV).

Now pause for just a moment. "In the beginning" here refers to the beginning of time, meaning God was preexistent. Some "experts" today would suggest that the universe, not a Divine Creator, was preexistent. But this is logically and chronologically impossible. The universe could not have created itself, as it would have to have already been in existence in order to do so. Whatever, or whoever, began space, time, and matter, must be timeless, space-less, and immaterial. In other words, in order to create the universe, the Creator must be preexistent to it. He must be outside the universe and not made from matter.

The Bible teaches that God existed before the beginning of time, matter, and life itself. He established everything we see. He is the source of all life.

The Bible begins with one God, revealed in three persons: God the Father, God the Son, and God the Holy Spirit. Simplified, there are not three gods, but one. Consider the chemical equation for water, H_2O. Water can be a solid (ice), a steam (gas), or a liquid, depending on the temperature variable. But the essence of all these is still H_2O. Thus, the Divine Being exists in one essence (God), but three Persons (Father, Son, Holy Spirit).

In Colossians chapter 1, we see the manifestation of God in Jesus the Son. Paul writes about Christ as Creator:

> He is the image of the invisible God, the firstborn of all creation. For by him all things were created, in heaven and on earth, visible and invisible, whether thrones or dominions or rulers or authorities—all things were created through him and for him. And he is before all things, and in him all things hold together. And he is the head of the body, the church. He is the beginning, the firstborn from the dead, that in everything he might be preeminent. For in him all the fullness of God was pleased to dwell, and through him to reconcile to himself all things, whether on earth or in heaven, making peace by the blood of his cross. (Colossians 1:15–20 ESV)

If you want to know what God is like, look at Jesus.

If you want to know what God is like, look at Jesus. By Him, all things were created. And Jesus is *before* all things." In other words, Jesus didn't just begin existing on Christmas morning. He existed from eternity past. He left heaven and came to earth and took on the form of a man. Paul goes on to say that in Christ all things hold together. In other words, when you study the forces of the universe, such as the distance of the Earth to the Sun, you discover that if the Earth were to come a little closer to the Sun, Earth and its inhabitants would instantly ignite and burn up. And if we drifted a little further away, we would freeze to death. Just a minor tilt, and the results would be catastrophic. So, what keeps the Earth in perfect orbit? The Bible says Jesus "holds all things together."

Why can you count on the forces of aerodynamics to consistently work when you are in an airplane? Jesus holds all things together. What about the cycles of food production, all the things that go on around us? You and I live in a world that can scare us sometimes. The United Nations published a report 10 years ago that said that in the next 10 years, the earth would increase by 2 degrees centigrade (35.6 Fahrenheit) and virtually be destroyed. But guess what? We're still here. You could sit around and think about "what ifs" all day. What if North Korea bombs us? What if Iran gets a nuclear bomb? What if an electromagnetic pulse .... ? Or you can simply say, "Lord, the world is too big for me to take care of. I am grateful that in You all things are held together."

In verse 20 of that same Colossians chapter, we see the Thread of Redemption that holds the Bible all together. It states that, "through him to reconcile to himself all things, whether on earth or in heaven, making peace by the blood of his cross" (Colossians 1:20).

So God created time. God created matter. God created life. He spoke, and creation appeared. I cannot imagine what it was like before Genesis 1:1. I cannot imagine a state of nothingness. Because nothingness is the absence of time, space, and matter. Yet an infinite God lives beyond these things.

Genesis also says that God created the first human beings, Adam and Eve, in the garden of Eden, located near the Tigris and Euphrates valley:

> Then the Lord God formed the man of dust from the ground and breathed into his nostrils the breath of life, and the man became a living creature. (Genesis 2:7 ESV)

You and I did not arbitrarily evolve from some primordial ooze with no purpose or destiny. We were *created*. When I toured the Smithsonian museum, studying the origins of man and cultural anthropology, I observed room after room containing skulls and bones, but nowhere in this great museum was any reference to God. The secular world in which you and I live, and in which our children are educated, does not explain mankind's beginning as the result of a Creator. Instead, it begins with a mindless, purposeless "Big Bang," an explosion of matter which birthed our universe and us. It takes more faith to believe that than it does to believe that there is an intelligent designer, and that a personal, intelligent God created us with purpose.

Man was created for relationship. But when man fell into sin in the Garden of Eden, everything changed.

Man was created for relationship. But when man fell into sin in the Garden of Eden, everything changed

> And the Lord God commanded the man, saying, "You may surely eat of every tree of the garden, but of the tree of the knowledge of good and evil you shall not eat, for in the day that you eat of it you shall surely die." (Genesis 2:16–17 ESV)

When Adam sinned, he didn't immediately die, *physically*. He lived on this earth a little while longer. However, he did die *spiritually* at that moment. "Death" in Scripture always means separation, and spiritually speaking, separation from God. Adam was separated from God at the moment of sin and he died physically many years later. Sin brings separation, and an interruption of relationship. So, Adam hid in shame and was driven from the garden. All this happened when Satan, the devil (also known as Lucifer, a fallen angel), fell from heaven because of his own sin. He then tempted Adam and Eve to follow him, and when they said yes to him using their own free will, that's when evil came into the world. And if you want a simple answer for why bad things happen to good people, why people die, why there are hurricanes, why there are wild fires, why there is destruction on the planet, and why there is rape and violence, it's because sin entered the world. And until the day when God removes all sin and sinners, sin will continue to affect the human race.

But here is something worth noting. When Adam and Eve were driven from the Garden, God did not send them out uncovered. The Bible says in Genesis 3:21 that "the Lord God made clothing from animal skins for Adam and his wife" (NLT).

Do you see the thread of redemption here? God didn't go to Bass Pro Shop to buy some animal skins. No, an animal actually lost its life. Now, you may not understand that part of the Bible. Why would God do such a thing? I will tell you why. It's because sin is serious business to God. So serious in fact that God requires the life of a living thing to pay the penalty for it. Hebrews 9:22 states, "without the shedding of blood there is no forgiveness of sins" (ESV).

So, this animal's blood being shed atoned for (or covered) the sins of Adam and Eve. And throughout the Old Testament, this blood covering happened through the shedding of the blood of an animal on a recurring basis as a foreshadowing of a future sacrificial death. It previewed the death of Christ, which offered ultimate and complete forgiveness.

And the rest of the Bible is about God's plan to restore relationship between Him and humankind.

4

A Chosen People

Moving from the book of beginnings, we see that the rest of the Old Testament tells us the story and history of the Jewish people, the nation of Israel. They are called God's "chosen people" for two reasons: 1. God chose this race to receive His Law, or moral standards, including the Ten Commandments. God's Law shows us how far we fall short of His righteous standards and requirements, convincing us that we need a Savior. And He established a covenant relationship with the Jews as well. 2. They were also chosen to be a part of the lineage of Jesus Christ. We forget sometimes that, though the Bible is not primarily a history book, it does contain a great deal of factual history. One example of this is the "family tree" of Jesus. When we look at the Genealogy of Jesus recorded in both Matthew and Luke, we see that His lineage is traced all the way back to the first man, Adam. Through the first man, Adam, sin came into the world. But through the "Second Adam," Jesus, reconciliation and salvation came (Romans 5:12–21).

But another way God demonstrated to the Jewish people that they needed a Savior was through the patriarchs. Patriarchs were like the "grandfathers of the faith," and it all began with a man named Abraham. The three major faiths of the world—Christianity, Judaism, and Islam— all look to Abraham as a significant person in their faith story. But from a New Testament perspective, Abraham also plays an important role. It is through his life that we learn that we cannot earn our way into heaven, but that salvation depends upon our placing faith in God and His provision for sin.

> It is through his [Abraham's] life that we learn that we cannot earn our way into heaven, but that salvation depends upon our placing faith in God and His provision for our sin.

That is why it depends on faith, in order that the promise may rest on grace and be guaranteed to all his offspring—not only to the adherent of the law but also to the one who shares the faith of Abraham, who is the father of us all.
(Romans 4:16 ESV)

Abraham teaches a lot about faith and grace. Grace is God's free gift to us. We don't get to heaven by being good, because we could never do enough good things to meet the requirements of heaven. We would have to achieve perfection in order to do this. Jesus said in John 3:16 that, "For God so loved the world, that he gave his only Son, that whoever believes in him should not perish but have eternal life."

So Abraham was a key Old Testament figure who showed us that we can't be good enough to get to heaven. He had a son named Isaac, also a central figure in salvation's narrative. In Genesis 22, we read about the binding of Isaac. It's the most graphic depiction in the Old Testament of a substitutionary sacrifice, as a lamb took the place of Isaac upon the altar. And that sacrifice foreshadowed, or previewed, the ultimate sacrifice of Christ.

Now Isaac had a "knucklehead" son named Jacob. Perhaps you can identify with making a few knucklehead decisions in your own life. But God eventually turned Jacob around, renaming him "Israel." And the nation that bears his name was made up of 12 tribes. From there, the story unfolds. The Jewish family grows, and then God supernaturally sends a famine into the world. That's bad, but God is able to use something bad and turn it into something good. Around this time, one of Israel's children, Joseph, is betrayed by his brothers and forcibly sent down into Egypt. Then, because Pharaoh has food, God brings the children of Israel from the Promised Land to Egypt. Joseph is eventually appointed to a high government position in Pharaoh's administration, and he effectually saves the world. The Jews are preserved, and they stay in Egypt. But over the next 300–400 years, they grow from 70 people into a nation of 1–2 million.

Sadly though, they are made into slaves, forced to build Pharaoh's pyramids.

But enter a man called Moses, who is sent by God to deliver them from bondage, proclaims to Pharaoh, "Let my people go!"

Through God's power, Moses brings 10 plagues, the last of which is the death of every first-born male in Egypt. But the Jewish males are spared through the inaugural practice of what became known as the *Passover*. This is another part of the thread of redemption weaving its way throughout the Scripture. In Exodus chapter 12, Moses says that each family must choose a lamb for a sacrifice: "They are to take some of the blood and smear it on the sides and top of the doorframes of the houses where they eat the animal" (v.7 NLT).

> "For this is the Lord's Passover. On that night I will pass through the land of Egypt and strike down every firstborn son and firstborn male animal in the land of Egypt. I will execute judgment against all the gods of Egypt, for I am the Lord! But the blood on your doorposts will serve as a sign, marking the houses where you are staying. When I see the blood, I will pass over you. This plague of death will not touch you when I strike the land of Egypt." (Exodus 12:11-13 NLT)

This marks the continuity between Genesis and Revelation, with Christ being the central figure and link between the two.

So what is the exact symbolism of all this? You may remember that when John the Baptist introduced Jesus at his baptism, he said: "Behold, the lamb of God, who takes away the sin of the world" (John 1:29 ESV). This marks the continuity between Genesis and Revelation, with Christ being the central figure and link between the two.

Once delivered out of Egypt by Moses, the Jewish people wander in the wilderness for close to 40 years. During this time, they get the law of Moses, the Ten Commandments. So you might be wondering, "What's the purpose of the Old Testament law for me as a New Testament believer?"

Galatians 3:24 tells us, "the law was our schoolmaster to bring us unto Christ, that we might be justified by faith" (KJV).

The Jews had a law code that covered everything from catfish to pork ribs, what you could and could not do on certain days, as well as an elaborate sacrificial system. And all this was given to show us we could never be good enough to go to heaven. Not one of us qualifies for entrance into Heaven. We desperately need God's gift of grace (Romans 3:10–12, 23; 5:8; 6:23).

Upon finally entering the Promised Land under Joshua, Israel is ruled by what's called a "Theocracy," which is a king and the priest, civil government and spiritual government coming together under God. We see Israel's great success under the kingdoms of David and Solomon, but then it all falls apart. For 700 years, from the beginning of Moses until the final exile, God's prophets warned that if they kept disobeying Him, there would come a day when God would judge them and they would be driven from the land. And that is exactly what happened. King Nebuchadnezzar came and took the children of Israel to Babylon. But the good news is that Jeremiah the prophet foretold that their captivity would only last 70 years. That's amazing, because that's exactly what happened.

No one today can accurately predict what will happen in 70 years. Some are saying that artificial intelligence will make human beings unnecessary, taking our jobs and making us obsolete. But at best, their claims are only educated guesses. They can't know for certain what will happen. But what Jeremiah said did come true. After 70 years, God raised up a pagan king named Cyrus who sent the Jews back to the Promised Land because he wanted to be blessed too.

That's where the latter part of the Old Testament starts winding down. The Jews come home and rebuild their temple and Jerusalem's walls, thanks to the leadership of men like Ezra and Nehemiah.

The Old Testament officially ends with the book of Malachi, one of the minor prophets. Malachi looks ahead in history, 400 years down the road, and prophecies about the Messiah's forerunner, John the Baptist. Then the Old Testament closes, and there is 400 years of silence until the New Testament opens its pages with the birth of Jesus Christ, Scripture's central figure.

5

The New Testament - Someone Has Come

Think about this. The New Testament makes up about 40% of the Bible. It has 27 books compared to the Old Testament's 39. The first four books are the Gospels: Matthew, Mark, Luke, and John. They tell the story of Jesus. Keep in mind that the Bible has been proven to be an accurate historical book. It's the most well-preserved book of antiquity. Many People today have no problem believing that Shakespeare's writings are an accurate account of what he wrote, or of virtually any other historical document. Their accuracy is almost never questioned. But in terms of preserved artifacts and copies, the Bible trumps every other book of antiquity 10,000 to 1. It is a historically accurate book that faithfully records the life, death, and resurrection of Jesus Christ.

After the Gospels, we see the book of Acts, which chronicles the beginning of the church and how Christianity began spreading all around the world. Then we have the Epistles (First and Second Corinthians, Galatians, Ephesians, etc.) written to various churches and individual believers. These letters also tell a story. They help Christians and churches correct their problems, while at the same time giving us sound doctrine, showing us what is true and worth believing. The Bible closes with the book of Revelation, which is a book primarily about the end times and the return of Jesus to planet Earth.

> It is a historically accurate book that faithfully records the life, death, and resurrection of Jesus Christ.

6

The Uniqueness of Jesus

The whole Bible is about Jesus, but the four Gospels detail His birth, life, and mission. Contrary to what you might think, "Christ" is not Jesus' last name. Jesus was a common name in that day, meaning "God is salvation." Many people were named Jesus. But "Christ" means "Messiah" or Savior. Jesus Christ is both God and man. 100% God and 100% man. I cannot fully explain that, but I believe it. He was born to a virgin named Mary. We don't know much about His early days (see Luke 2:52), but we know that His public ministry begins when He was about 30 years old, and it only lasts about three years. His ministry has had such a great effect on humanity that today, in a world with about seven billion people, over two billion call themselves "Christians." All because of this one Man's ministry, just three years on earth. His miracles attest to His divine nature. And though He had thousands of disciples, He chose just 12 to be in His inner circle. It was to them that He would entrust the task of proclaiming the good news (Gospel) to the entire known world.

After rising from the dead, Jesus spent about 40 days teaching his disciples, after which He ascended back to heaven. The Bible tells us that right now Jesus is seated at the right hand of God the Father, waiting for the word to come back to earth. One day, time as we know it will be no more. Christ is returning, and when He does, it will change everything.

Look at what Jesus said in Mark 14:62:

"And you will see the Son of Man seated in the place of power at God's right hand and coming on the clouds of heaven." (NLT)

Jesus' moral teachings...literally shaped the foundation of Western Civilization in terms of ethics and values.

Jesus is not coming back as a baby in a manger. He is coming back as King of kings and Lord of lords. That's because He is God.

Jesus' moral teachings, like we read about in the Sermon on the Mount, literally shaped the foundation of Western Civilization in terms of ethics and values. Even time itself was divided by His birth. For centuries, we used B.C. (Before Christ), and A.D., a Latin term meaning "in the

Year of our Lord." But now secularists are dropping those abbreviations, using instead B.C.E. (Before the Common Era) and C.E. (Common Era). Mankind does its best to try and rid the world of the Gospel message. Just like Pharaoh tried to get rid of the Jewish children. But he couldn't stop Moses. They couldn't keep Jesus in the ground. And they won't be able to stop His gospel.

It really doesn't matter how powerful the United Nations is, how powerful the Republicans or Democrats are, or even who's on our Supreme Court. None of them can thwart God's plan. The Bible says that before Jesus Christ, every knee will bow and every tongue confess that Jesus Christ is Lord, to the glory of God the Father (Philippians 2:9–11). That being true, wouldn't it make sense to bow before Him now as Savior instead of having to bow before Him then as Judge?

Jesus talked about the two great commandments. We can summarize them in this way:

1. "Love the Lord your God with all of your heart and with all your soul and with all your mind and with all your strength" (Mark 12:30 NIV). This goes way beyond merely attending church once a week. And it's more than trying to keep a set of rules. It means having a real *relationship* with God.

2. The second commandment is to "love your neighbor as yourself" (Matthew 22:39). We could solve most of the world's problems if we simply embraced those two commands. We could end the violence and virtually put the prison system out of business if humanity would only turn to Christ. Pornography, sex trafficking, sexual harassment, rape, racism, murder, and all the evils of our culture could be

radically reduced. All this, if we would simply listen to the Savior's words:

"Love God. Love others."

But in order to do this, the Bible says we must first experience the salvation God offers to each one of us. In Matthew 20, Jesus said:

> "The Son of Man will be delivered over to the chief priests and scribes, and they will condemn him to death and deliver him over to the Gentiles
> to be mocked and flogged and crucified, and he
> will be raised on the third day" (vv. 18–19 ESV).

Jesus knew He came to this earth for one reason. Beyond just showing us how to live, He came to be the Passover Lamb and to pay the penalty for your sin and mine. He says in John 14:6 (ESV):

> **"I am the way, and the truth, and the life. No one comes to the Father except through me."**

Note the definitive article, *the*, repeated three times. No other religious teacher offers the exclusive pathway to heaven. And no other religious leader backed up such words by rising from the dead. The problem is that our sin separates us from God and the life that He offers. But we have rejected His gracious offer. Our sin, and love of self, keep us far from God. We took His commandments off of our school walls and have rejected His moral standards in our culture. We would rather have policemen and guard dogs and metal detectors in our schools, than have God's wise commandments to invest in the hearts of our children. And look where that approach has brought us. This is the underlying problem of our society. Man wants to be his own God. And it is that attitude and spirit that says, "No one will tell me what to do. I make my own rules." This is what is destroying us as individuals and as a nation. If we continue to reject and run from Jesus, our lives will only lead to ruin. But if we bow our wills to His and put our faith in Him, we will experience rebirth, redemption, and a renewed life.

Jesus gave us this great hope in John 11:25 (ESV): "I am the resurrection and the life. Whoever believes in me, though he die, yet shall he live." Only Jesus.

No other religious teacher offers the exclusive pathway to heaven. And no other religious leader backed up such words by rising from the dead.

7

What Exactly is the "Church?"

The amazing Bible continues in the New Testament book of Acts, which tells the story of the Church's early history. It began on the Day of Pentecost when the Holy Spirit fell on Jewish believers in the upper room in Jerusalem. Peter was the primary voice and leader of the newly-birthed church. And the epicenter of its expansion was Jerusalem. Acts focuses on the Jews in chapters 1 through 11, but around chapter 12 or 13, the focus shifts. Paul becomes the great Apostle to the Gentiles (or non-Jews), and the central city is now Antioch. The gospel expands to all of humanity, not just the Jews. And the rest of the New Testament unfolds the story of what originally began in the book of Acts.

If I could give you four words that describe and summarize the Book of Acts and the Epistles, and that encompass the spirit of the New Testament, they would be: Mission, Message, Means, and Methods.

The New Testament Church had a *Mission*, commonly called the "Great Commission." Jesus said:

> "Go therefore and make disciples of all nations, baptizing them in the name of the Father and of the Son and of the Holy Spirit, teaching them to observe all that I have commanded you." Matthew 28:19–20 (ESV)

This is what the Church is all about. When Jesus left this planet, He personally commissioned every Christian, both those portrayed in the pages of Scripture as well as those who have come to faith in Jesus since that time. **The mission is to bring others to Christ.**

Second, the New Testament Church had a *Message:* **the Good News that Christ was crucified, died, was buried, and rose from the dead** (1 Corinthians 15:3–4). I heard that good news on August 15, 1976. I had been raised in church, but I wasn't a Christian. That's because going to church won't make you a Christian any more than going into the water makes you a fish. But it was on that day when I humbled myself, as I read the Gideon New Testament, that I was convinced and began a new life. The Bible's *words* of life led me to the *Lord* of life! I learned that God offers forgiveness through Christ. This was the good news for me, a sinner. And it was, and is, *the* message of the church.

So, the church had a Mission and a Message. But they also had a *Means* as well. And it's the same as ours, the **power and gifts of the Holy Spirit.** Jesus told His disciples in Acts 1:8 (ESV), "You will receive power when the Holy Spirit has come upon you, and you will be my witnesses." In the rest of the pages of the Bible you see men and women and even young boys and girls under the influence of the Spirit. And that's how the gospel went forward and spread all over the known world.

Lastly, their *Method* was quite simple. It was **"preaching," or heralding the good news of the gospel. Winning souls, making disciples and planting churches.** That was it. Their mandate determined their method. You see, every church member is a missionary, taking Christ's message of salvation wherever you go. And if it was good enough for them, it ought to be good enough for us too.

Church really isn't complicated. All we have to do is to simply consecrate our hearts towards the task of spreading the good news of Jesus.

Every church member is a missionary, taking Christ's message of salvation wherever you go.

8

Revelation - Someone is Coming Again

The Bible closes with the climactic book of Revelation, which tells us about the future. Imagine you had a sure bet on where the stock market was going every day of the year. If so, you could make a lot of money. If you could just know where the DOW is going to be on January 31st, you could become wealthy beyond your wildest imagination. But to do so, you would have to be able to foretell the future. And that's exactly what the book of Revelation does. It was originally given to the apostle John as a vision from Jesus Christ Himself. It is a book written in two time frames. Though it was written in the era of the Early Church, specifically to seven churches in Asia Minor, its message concerns us as well, for it reveals what's coming to this world. The book of Revelation talks about the Antichrist, the Mark of the Beast and the One World Government. All this should concern you. During the time known as the Tribulation Period, God will send a series of horrific judgments upon the earth and upon unbelievers.

Revelation also says there is coming a day when no one will be able to buy or sell without this "mark of the beast." And those without Christ will not be able to escape this prophetic end-times phenomenon. It is coming. There is already microchip technology available and being implanted into the hands of people. I am not suggesting that is the mark of the beast, but I am assuring you that one day the antichrist will rule the world. He will be in charge, and he will unleash a great persecution against Jews and Christians. The book of Revelation is a book filled with horrible death for many believers. All because they chose Christ over antichrist.

The Bible says in Revelation 12:11 (ESV), "And they have conquered him (the devil) by the blood of the Lamb and by the word of their testimony, for they loved not their lives even unto death."

You see, earth is not our home. Our home is yet to come in a real place called heaven. Revelation in the New Testament tells us about the Rapture of the church and the Second Coming of Christ (1 Thessalonians 4:13–18; Revelation 19:11–21). The devil that tempted Eve is the same devil that will be judged and ultimately cast into the lake of fire. The book of Revelation closes with the end of time, the final judgment, and the reality of heaven and hell.

I would be unloving if I did not tell you about what the Bible says about Judgment Day. In Revelation 20:11–12 (ESV), John the Revelator describes his vision: "I saw a great white throne and him who was seated on it... And I saw the dead, great and small, standing before the throne."

Every unbeliever will be there. And it will be a terrifying day. Rich and poor. Famous and insignificant. Politicians and plumbers. Celebrities and socialites. Every person throughout history who refused to bow the knee to Christ will appear before God's Great White Throne. And without Jesus as your Savior, you will be there too.

Verse 12 continues, stating that "books were opened." These books recorded our lives. Everything we thought, everything we said and did is recorded. How could that be? Because an infinite God has been watching. Like Siri and GPS knowing how far it is to our next destination, artificial intelligence today can tell us how to navigate our way across the country with great precision. But Almighty God eclipses any supercomputer or artificial intelligence. Put simply, He *knows*.

> Every person throughout history who refused to bow the knee to Christ will appear before God's Great White Throne. And without Jesus as your Savior, you will be there too.

Scripture also says here that, "Then another book was opened, which is the book of life. And the dead were judged by what was written in the books, according to what they had done" (v. 12). That is a really bad day if you don't know

Christ. "And if anyone's name was not found written in the book of life, he was thrown into the lake of fire" (v. 15). Friend, believe me when I say that hell is a real place. But the good news is that God doesn't want anyone to go there. Only those that have rejected him will be thrown into this lake of fire.

The Bible says in Revelation 21, in one of the last chapters in the Bible, that John the Revelator saw a picture of a new heaven and a new earth. John viewed a city like a new Jerusalem coming down to the earth.

> And I heard a loud voice from the throne saying, "Behold, the dwelling place of God is with man. He will dwell with them, and they will be his people, and God himself will be with them as their God. He will wipe away every tear from their eyes, and death shall be no more, neither shall there be mourning, nor crying, nor pain anymore, for the former things have passed away."
> (Revelation 21:3–4 esv)

Back in Genesis, when God walked with Adam in the cool of the day, they had sweet fellowship. Now, at the end of time, once again God is with His people face to face. Because of this reconciliation, all is well once again. Think about it. No more doctors' appointments. No more cancer or pain. No more mosquitos or snakes. No more crime, evil, violence, heartache, or death. The former things of this life are officially gone.

The very last verse of the Bible, Revelation 22:20 (esv), gives us a hopeful message: "He who testifies to these things says, 'Surely I am coming soon.'" And John responded as we will: "Amen. Come, Lord Jesus!"

9

So, What Now?

You may be wondering what all this has to do with you. You may be thinking, "What's the point of it all for me? What difference does it make?"

James tells us to, "... get rid of all the filth and evil in your lives, and humbly accept the word God has planted in your hearts, for it has the power to save your souls." (James 1:21 NLT)

Simply put, if you choose today to believe in Jesus and what He did on the cross for you 2000 years ago, then you can have your sins forgiven and the assurance of knowing that you will go to heaven when you die. Instead of following your own desires like Adam and Eve, why not turn to Jesus and simply believe, committing your life to Him. That's what the Bible calls "repentance." It's a commitment to Jesus to follow Him the rest of your life. But words aren't enough. It's much more than just saying a prayer; It's a heart commitment.

James 1:22 says, "But don't just listen to God's word. You must do what it says. Otherwise, you are only fooling yourselves." (NLT) But if you do what it says and don't forget what you heard, then God will bless you for doing it.

Faith in Christ brings salvation. Jesus Christ promises to save your soul and give you eternal life. Is that what you want? If so, why not tell Him that right now, and begin a relationship with the One who wrote the AMAZING BIBLE!

Simply put, if you choose today to believe
in Jesus and what He did on the
cross for you 2000 years ago,
then you can have your sins forgiven
and the assurance of knowing that
you will go to heaven when you die.

HOW TO KNOW JESUS CHRIST AS YOUR PERSONAL SAVIOR

The Bible is the foundation for Christianity. It contains the answers to all of life's vital questions and changes the very lens of the worldview through which we view reality. Most importantly, it teaches us how to have a true, meaningful relationship with God.

These verses illustrate God's plan for your salvation:

GOD LOVES YOU
For God so loved the world, that he gave his only son, that whoever believes in him should not perish but have eternal life. – John 3:16

But God shows his love for us in that while we were still sinners, Christ died for us. – Romans 5:8

ALL ARE SINNERS
For all have sinned and fall short of the glory of God. – Romans 3:23

As it is written: "none is righteous, no, not one" – Romans 3:10

GOD'S REMEDY FOR SIN

For the wages of sin is death; but the free gift of God is eternal life in Christ Jesus our Lord. – Romans 6:23

But to all who did receive him, who believed in his name, he gave the right to become children of God. – John 1:12

ALL MAY BE SAVED

Behold, I stand at the door and knock. If anyone hears my voice and opens the door, I come in to him and eat with him, and he with me. – Revelation 3:20

For "everyone who calls on the name of the Lord will be saved." – Romans 10:13

But these are written so that you may believe that Jesus is the Christ, the Son of God, and that by believing you may have life in his name. – John 20:31

PRAY

"God, I confess that I am a sinner and I am in need of salvation. I believe Jesus died on the cross for my sins and rose again to bring me new life. I ask You to forgive me and come into my life. Today, I choose to follow You as my Lord and Savior. Amen."

Sign: _____

Date: _____

*Used with permission from www.gideons.org

41

ASSURANCE OF YOUR SALVATION

Assurance for the believer comes directly from God's Word. The Gospel tells us that because Christ died for us, anyone who trusts in Him may know that their sins have been forgiven, once and for all.

Because, if you confess with your mouth that Jesus is Lord and believe in your heart that God raised him from the dead, you will be saved. – Romans 10:9

Truly, truly, I say to you, whoever hears my word and believes him who sent me has eternal life. He does not come into judgment, but has passed from death to life. – John 5:24

WHAT DO I DO NOW?

1. Read your Bible every day and talk to God in prayer.
2. Become an active part of a Bible-believing local church.
3. Send a text to 97000 and type "RESTORED" to receive 10 short videos about spiritual growth.
4. Follow me and watch my daily videos for spiritual encouragement on, "Facebook, Instagram, TikTok, Lemon8, and Truth Social. Search for Pastor John Miller, Pastor John H Miller, or gardening pastor.
5. Download the Church on the Rock app by searching for COTR TXK. You will find helpful sermons and a daily Bible reading plan.